# Shred Diet Recipes:

## Burn Fat and Lose Weight Easily

By

Valerie Alston

# Table of Contents

Introduction ................................................................... 6

1. Breakfast Recipes ..................................................... 7

    Red Pears and Blueberries Breakfast Smoothie ............... 7

    Peanut Butter and Banana Smoothies .............................. 8

    Breakfast Pizza ............................................................. 9

    Chocolate Protein Breakfast Shake ................................ 10

    Peach and Strawberry Breakfast Smoothie .................... 11

    Rich Berries Breakfast Smoothie ................................... 12

    Simple Breakfast Egg Salad .......................................... 13

    Fruity Energy Blast Breakfast Smoothie ........................ 14

    Banana and Strawberry Creamy Smoothie .................... 15

2. Main Meal Recipes .................................................. 16

    The Ultimate Chicken Noodle Soup .............................. 16

    Rice Stew ................................................................... 18

    Grilled Shrimp in Skewers ........................................... 19

    Grilled Chicken Recipe ................................................ 20

    Chicken Tortilla Recipe ............................................... 21

    Tender Grilled Pork Chop with Sweet Potatoes and Asparagus .................................................................. 22

    Quick Tuna Salad Recipe ............................................. 24

    Shredded Spaghetti Using Lean Red Meat ................... 25

Shredded Green Salad Festival ......................................... 26

3. Snack Recipes ................................................................ 27

    Crispy Vegetables with Guacamole Dip .......................... 27

    Baked Sweet Potato with Salsa ....................................... 28

    Olives Stuffed with Blue Cheese ..................................... 29

    Tuna on Wheat Toast ..................................................... 30

Final Words ....................................................................... 31

Thank You Page ................................................................. 33

Shred Diet Recipes: Burn Fat and Lose Weight Easily

By Valerie Alston

© Copyright 2014 Valerie Alston

Reproduction or translation of any part of this work beyond that permitted by section 107 or 108 of the 1976 United States Copyright Act without permission of the copyright owner is unlawful. Requests for permission or further information should be addressed to the author.

This publication is designed to provide accurate and authoritative information in regard to the subject matter covered. This work is sold with the understanding that the publisher is not engaged in rendering legal, accounting, or other professional services. If legal advice or other expert assistance is required, the services of a competent professional person should be sought.

First Published, 2014

Printed in the United States of America

## Introduction

The secret of the Shred diet is a combination of a low gastrointestinal diet which eases work on the digestive system, efficient meal spacing so that your body will be able to digest the foods you eat faster and using meal replacements. In this diet, you will be constantly eating which is ironic in a weight loss plan.

This diet plan also introduces a new concept called diet confusion which is basically tricking the body to increase its performance to be able to lose weight. The Shred diet also recommends using a personalized workout plan to help lose weight more effectively.

Recipes found in this book will help you to follow the diet.

# 1. Breakfast Recipes

## Red Pears and Blueberries Breakfast Smoothie

This is a simple breakfast smoothie that is easy on the digestive tract and will provide you with all the nutrients that you will need during the most important meal of the day. You will need about 1 ½ cups of red pears, a cup of frozen blueberries, a cup of plain low-fat yoghurt, a teaspoon of white sugar and crushed ice or 6 ice cubes.

Wash the pears and rinse the blueberries. Cut the pears into small pieces. Place these fruits in a blender or a juicer. If you are using a blender, place the pears and blueberries in and then blend. After achieving a smooth mixture add the sugar and then pulse for another five seconds. Finally add the crushed ice. If you are using a juicer, drop the pears first and then the berries. Place sugar in the glass and stir; drop the ice cubes in.

## Peanut Butter and Banana Smoothies

If you are looking for something sweet but at the same time easy on the stomach in the morning then you will love to prepare and drink this easy breakfast smoothie. You will need ½ small ripe banana, ½ cup of fat-free plain yoghurt, 2 tablespoons of unsalted peanut butter, ½ cup of fat free milk, a teaspoon of honey and about 6 ice cubes.

Remove the banana peel and slice the banana in half. Place this in a blender; add the yoghurt and the unsalted peanut butter. Blend until you get a smooth consistency. Add the milk and honey last. Mix for another 5 seconds and then place the contents in a tall glass with ice cubes and serve.

## Breakfast Pizza

This is a fast and easy recipe that you can prepare in less than a minute. It is very light and easy on the digestive tract since it contains easy to digest ingredients that will provide you with energy that you need in the morning. You will need a whole wheat English muffin, a tablespoon of tomato sauce, a tablespoon of low-fat cheese and a tablespoon of parmesan cheese.

Simply prepare your English muffin by cutting it in half and spreading tomato sauce on each half. Spread the cheese over the sauce and top with parmesan cheese. Broil your pizza or place in an oven toaster. Cut into halves and then serve with an additional sprinkle of cheese on top.

## Chocolate Protein Breakfast Shake

Possibly the best way to add protein to your day is to drink a healthy protein shake but this shake is totally different. Instead of just using protein powder you will also add a banana and additional milk to make it creamier and healthier. You will need a scoop of protein shake (recommended is the Body Fortress Chocolate Super Advanced Whey variety), unsweetened dry cocoa powder, a medium size banana, pure almond milk about ¼ cup and ¼ cup of non-fat skim milk. You may either use ice cubes or crushed ice for this shake recipe.

Chop the banana into small pieces and then place in a blender. Add the milk ingredients and then mix; after you get a smooth consistency add the dry ingredients. Add the ice cubes or crushed ice last. Serve in a tall glass; this only makes one serving.

## Peach and Strawberry Breakfast Smoothie

Peaches and strawberries are great sources of vitamin C, sodium and fiber. These fruits are also very low in cholesterol and fat. You will also enjoy its fruity and light taste that will energize you in the morning. You will need ¼ cup of non-fat skim milk, ½ cup of non-fat vanilla-flavored yoghurt (recommended Dannon Light yoghurt variety), ½ cup of fresh strawberries, ½ cup of yellow cling peaches in light syrup and 4 ice cubes or a cup of crushed ice.

Cut the peaches in half; remove the top part of the strawberries. Place these in a blender and mix for about 10 seconds. Add the non-fat milk and then the yoghurt. Mix for 5 seconds and then add the ice cubes or crushed ice. Serve in a tall glass; you may place strawberry bits on top of the mixture just before you serve it.

## Rich Berries Breakfast Smoothie

This is a delicious and rich breakfast smoothie that is composed of two varieties of berries but you may also create your own recipe using your favorite berries. You will get a healthy supply of fiber, sodium and protein from this healthy breakfast smoothie. You will need ¼ cup of fresh blueberries, ¼ cup of strawberries, ¼ cup of blackberries, 6 oz. of light blueberry yoghurt, ½ cup of non-fat skim milk, freshly squeezed lemon juice and 4 ice cubes or crushed ice.

Wash the berries carefully and then place these in a blender; mix until you get a smooth consistency. Add the skim milk, yoghurt and the lemon juice blend this once more and then place crushed ice and pulse for another 5 seconds. You may also pour the mixture in a glass with ice cubes if you do not prefer to use crushed ice. This makes only one serving.

## Simple Breakfast Egg Salad

This is a simple and easy to make recipe since it only has three ingredients. In a Shred diet, the simpler the better so that your digestive tract will be able to digest food easier. This recipe provides proteins, fiber, sodium and cholesterol. You will need a large egg, a teaspoon of low-fat mayonnaise and a slice of wheat bread.

Hard boil the egg. Crack open the egg and slice it into small pieces or you may use a fork to press the egg and then place this in a small bowl. Mix the mayonnaise in and then place on a slice of wheat bread. You may season the salad with salt and freshly ground black pepper before placing on the wheat bread slice.

## Fruity Energy Blast Breakfast Smoothie

Fruits are perfect during breakfast since these provide a healthy supply of vitamins, minerals and fiber. For this breakfast smoothie you will need a cup of fresh strawberries, ¼ cup of fresh blueberries, a medium kiwi fruit, a medium-sized banana, a serving of light, fat-free yoghurt (recommended Harvest Peach Light Yoghurt), ¼ cup of light orange juice (recommended Minute Maid Light Orange Juice with 50% Less Calories) and about 7 ice cubes or a cup of crushed ice.

Wash the fruits before using them. Remove the skin of the kiwi fruit and cut it into small pieces; cut the banana into small slices and then discard any unripe berries. Place all the fruits in a blender and then mix completely. Add the yoghurt and orange juice, mix until you get a smooth consistency. Add the crushed ice and then pulse for another 5 seconds. Pour in a tall glass. You may place small bits of strawberries and blueberries on top to make a crunchy smoothie.

## Banana and Strawberry Creamy Smoothie

This is a smoothie that will energize you in the morning with huge amounts of protein, vitamin C, sodium and fiber. You will also love the creamy strawberry goodness that will linger in your tongue all morning. You will need a medium size frozen banana, ½ cup of frozen strawberries, 1.5 tablespoons of flaxseeds, a serving of non-fat vanilla yoghurt (recommended Dannon Light & Fit Non-fat Vanilla Yoghurt), and ¼ cup of non-fat skim milk and ¼ tablespoons of honey.

Wash the strawberries just before freezing them. In the morning, place frozen berries in a blender, cut the banana into small pieces and then place these in a blender along with the flaxseeds. Add the milk and then blend until you get a smooth consistency. Add the honey and yoghurt and then blend once more. Pour in a glass with ice or add crushed ice cubes and then mix for another 5 seconds.

## 2. Main Meal Recipes

### The Ultimate Chicken Noodle Soup

Chicken noodle soup is more than chicken broth but it should be made of ingredients that contain all the nutrients that the body needs during the middle of the day. This is a Shred chicken noodle soup especially from the creator of the diet plan. You will need about 1 ½ cups of wide egg noodles, a tablespoon of butter, ½ cup of onion, and ½ cup of celery, ¾ cup of carrots, 1 ½ cups of cooked chicken meat (breast part), 6 cups of chicken broth, 1 ½ cups of vegetable broth, ¼ cup of water, and ½ teaspoon of dried basil leaves. ½ teaspoon of dried oregano leaves, a teaspoon of chicken flavoured seasoning and a teaspoon of salt.

Cook the egg noodles according to package instructions or you may boil a pot of water with 2 tablespoons of salt. Boil your noodles for 7 minutes and then drain and place in a large bowl to set aside. Place a large soup pot and then melt the butter; place the onions and the celery and then cook until flavorful and the onions and celery are softer but do not overcook the vegetables. Add the pieces of chicken breast and then cook for a minute and then add the broth, water, carrots and the seasoning. Cook for about 5 minutes and then add the spices, salt and pepper. Boil everything and then reduce the heat and cook for about 10 minutes or until the carrot pieces are soft and the chicken pieces are easy to flake with a fork. Serve in a small bowl with a dash of spices on top of the soup.

## Rice Stew

Main meals in a Shred diet have to contain low calories but huge amounts of nutrients. This is a meal that you can prepare in less than 5 minutes and contains less than 200 calories, sodium, dietary fiber and protein. You will need a cup of cooked brown rice, about 8 ounces of cooked chicken breast or canned chicken flakes, a cup of sweet corn, a cup of black beans, ¼ cup of chicken broth, a teaspoon of barbecue sauce and a ¼ cup of onion chopped into very small pieces.

Use a large stir fry pan and then place a small amount of oil and cook the chopped onion until it is translucent. Add the barbecue sauce and the chicken broth and bring to a boil. Add the black beans and the corn and then cook for a minute. Add the brown rice and the cooked chicken flakes and then mix. Ensure that the sauce, beans and corn are evenly distributed in the rice; cook for 20 minutes on medium heat. This recipe will make about 4 servings of one cup of rice each.

## Grilled Shrimp in Skewers

This is a shrimp recipe that is perfect for lunch or dinner but takes a few minutes to prepare. This recipe is a good source of rich protein and minerals that will sustain you as you indulge in a Shred diet plan. You will need 40 large raw shrimps, freshly ground pepper and light oil spray. For the sauce you will need about 2 tablespoons of light mayonnaise, 2 tablespoons of scallions and a tablespoon of sweet chili sauce. You will also need wooden skewers (soak this in water for at least 30 minutes) or you may use metal grilling skewers instead.

Clean, devein and remove the shells of your shrimps and then place them in skewers about 4 to 5 shrimps in one skewer. Season this with ground pepper and set aside. Chop the scallions into small pieces. Combine the mayonnaise, chopped scallions and sweet chili sauce in a small bowl. Prepare your grill by heating it to medium heat and lightly oil it with the light oil spray. Place the shrimps over the grill and baste these with the sauce regularly. Cook each side for 6 to 8 minutes. You can tell that the shrimps are cooked when these look opaque and pinkish. Serve this with the rest of the sauce and a dash of freshly ground pepper on top.

## Grilled Chicken Recipe

Chicken is easy to cook plus it is tender and very juicy. About 100 grams of chicken contains only 119 calories, 21 grams of protein and minimal fat. You can therefore indulge in different chicken recipes for as long as you are in a Shred diet. This is a grilled chicken recipe using 100 grams of chicken breast, salt, ground pepper, a tablespoon of freshly squeezed lemon and two cloves of garlic.

Chop the garlic into small pieces and combine with the lemon juice. Season both sides of the chicken breast with salt and pepper and set aside. Prepare the grill by placing it on medium heat; slightly grease the grill with a light spray and then when the grill is hot, place the chicken breast. Baste with the lemon and garlic mixture often. Cook the chicken about 10 minutes on each side but turn it very often to prevent charring or burning, baste this with the lemon and garlic mixture every time you turn it.

## Chicken Tortilla Recipe

Another chicken recipe that will certainly provide you with protein energy for lunch and even for dinner. This recipe provides you with proteins for energy, whole wheat tortillas for fiber and spinach and carrots for vitamins and minerals. You will need 100 grams of chicken breast cooked, two or three tortilla pieces, a medium size carrot and a handful of spinach leaves. You also need a medium size onion, salt and pepper to taste and low fat cheese.

Flake the chicken breast and set these aside in a small bowl. Chop the onions and the carrots into very small pieces. Wash the spinach leaves and then cut into very small pieces too. Grate the cheese and set these aside as well. Arrange your tortillas in a plate; place a tortilla and then add the chicken flakes, onions, carrots and then top these with grated cheese. Serve with a drizzle of olive oil or low fat dressing on top.

## Tender Grilled Pork Chop with Sweet Potatoes and Asparagus

This is a complete meal that will certainly help you get shredded. It contains huge amounts of protein from the pork chop and vitamins and minerals from asparagus and sweet potatoes. You will need extra time to prepare this meal since you need to completely cook your chops and potatoes. You will need a medium size pork chop, a sweet potato, a cup of asparagus and salt and pepper to taste.

Prepare your grill by heating it to medium heat and spraying the grates with low fat oil spray. Season your pork chop with salt and pepper on each side; you may also use a teaspoon of lemon and garlic to make the meat more flavorful, set this aside. Clean and brush the sweet potato and the asparagus. Boil the sweet potato until it is very tender to eat. You will grill your asparagus so spray it lightly with oil. Place the chop on the grill and turn it once every five minutes. Both sides should be completely cooked but not charred for at least 10 minutes on each side. Place the asparagus on the top most part of the grill or if you only have a one layer grill, place these on the edge of the grill. Cook the asparagus until these are tender. When the pork chop is ready, arrange these on a plate along with the cooked sweet potato and asparagus stalks. Place low fat butter on top of the potato or on the asparagus stalks along with freshly ground pepper on top before serving.

## Quick Tuna Salad Recipe

Tuna is an excellent source of protein and has high antioxidants and nutrients for healthy brain development. Tuna is best cooked fresh but if you do not have access to a fresh supply then simply choose tuna in water in a can. You will need a can of tuna in water, a teaspoon of balsamic vinegar, ½ cup of cooked black beans, salt and pepper to taste.

You will need to drain the tuna in water really well and separate the flakes in a small bowl. Place the cooked black beans in the tuna flakes along with the vinegar. Mix these very well and then add salt and pepper. This is a recipe that will work with a slice of wheat bread or ½ cup of brown rice.

## Shredded Spaghetti Using Lean Red Meat

Lean red meat will provide you with proteins and minerals while you are on a Shred diet. And most of all, this recipe is also easy to cook. It will only take you less than 5 minutes to cook. You will need 5oz of cooked lean red meat, 1 medium size red bell pepper, and ½ cup of mushrooms and a cup of spaghetti sauce. You can choose what noodles you want to use as long as these are wheat, rice or egg noodles. Cook noodles according to package instructions.

Cut the lean meat into small pieces and set aside. Wash the red bell peppers and then chop these into small pieces. Chop mushrooms into small pieces as well. Heat the spaghetti sauce in a medium size saucepan and then bring to a boil. Add the red peppers and mushrooms and cook for about 15 minutes. Add the red meat and cook for another 30 minutes. Stir as you cook to prevent the sauce from sticking on the pan. Top these on your noodles and then garnish with shredded low fat cheese and mushrooms.

## Shredded Green Salad Festival

Vegetables are a part of every Shred diet. You may indulge in veggies as much as you want in a week and if you cannot find fresh veggies from your supermarket then you may use canned or frozen vegetables instead. For this recipe you will need a medium size tomato, half a head of cabbage, lettuce, green beans, spinach or kale.

Wash your veggies in running water and discard any wilted leaves, cut these into bite sized pieces and the tomato must be cut into smaller pieces. In a large salad bowl, place all the ingredients together and then toss. Drizzle with a light salad dressing or extra virgin olive oil. You may garnish this with cooked corn bits or green beans.

## 3. Snack Recipes

### Crispy Vegetables with Guacamole Dip

Shred snacks are simple and very easy to prepare. You can make this crispy vegetable snack in a minute if you have guacamole handy at home. But if you do not then you may need to make some; you will need 3 avocados, a small lime, a teaspoon of salt, a ½ cup of diced onion, 2 tablespoons of cilantro, 2 tomatoes and a dash of cayenne pepper. For the crispy veggies, select your vegetables carefully; you may choose from celery stalks, carrots, cucumbers or broccoli.

To make the guacamole dip, mash the avocadoes in a bowl and then mix the lime juice, salt and the cayenne pepper. Chop the cilantro, onions, tomatoes and the garlic into very small pieces and then add to the avocado and spices mixture. Blend everything until you get a smooth consistency. You may serve this immediately or place in the refrigerator for a few minutes before serving. Wash your crispy vegetables beforehand; cut the cucumbers, carrots and celery stalks into easy to dip and bite pieces. Remove cauliflower florets from the main stalk and them steam this for a few minutes before serving them. In a platter, arrange the veggies along the sides and place the guacamole dip in the middle.

## Baked Sweet Potato with Salsa

This is another low calorie snack that will fill you up and prevent you from overeating during lunch or dinner. Sweet potatoes are excellent sources of vitamins, magnesium, potassium and sodium. You will need two small sweet potatoes, salt and pepper and a tablespoon of salsa sauce.

Heat your oven to 350 degrees Fahrenheit. Wash sweet potatoes carefully in running water and then place in a baking pan. Cut open a small portion on the top part of the sweet potato and then let this bake for about 20 minutes. You can tell that the sweet potato is cooked when the peel is easy to remove from the potato. Serve with a dash of pepper and salt plus a small amount of salsa sauce on top of the potato.

## Olives Stuffed with Blue Cheese

Olives are rich sources of calories, antioxidants, sodium, potassium, fiber and iron. This is a very easy recipe that calls for only two ingredients; you can make stuffed olives for sacks or as finger foods for a party. You will need about 5 to 7 pieces of green olives and a tablespoon of blue cheese.

Prepare the olives by removing the middle part. Place blue cheese in each olive and then place in a small plate. This goes well with lemonade or unsweetened ice tea.

## Tuna on Wheat Toast

This is an easy snack recipe that will provide additional proteins, vitamins and minerals in between meals. You will need a can of tuna in water, a tablespoon of mayonnaise and a slice of wheat bread. Drain the tuna in water and then place the flakes of tuna in a small bowl. Add the mayonnaise and then mix completely. Toast the wheat bread and then cut diagonally to get two triangular slices of toasted wheat bread. Place the tuna salad on the toasted bread and then serve.

## Final Words

The Shred diet is all about modifying your regular diet plan into a completely new one without many changes in the food you eat. You may have noticed that most of the foods that are included in the diet plan are foods that you love to eat every day. The core of Shred is to eat fewer calories per meal to help you burn calories faster. And since the diet is all about minimizing your calorie consumption you will never feel hungry even though this is so since you will be required to eat more often compared to other diets that recommend you fast and abstain from the foods that you love to eat. Therefore you will never even feel there is a stark change in your diet plan when you are using Shred and most of all you can include this in your weight loss plan anytime.

With a Shred diet you will be able to have the body that you have always dreamed of in a matter of a few weeks. You will be able to lose weight and reduce dress sizes as you get a trimmer and healthier figure. With the Shred diet you will also be able to reduce some of the most common medical conditions and illnesses related to obesity like cardiovascular diseases, high blood pressure, high cholesterol levels and even prevent diabetes. Shred diet recipes may be used as a part of your daily meals even when you have successfully reduced your weight. By extending your Shred diet use you can maintain your trim figure and reduce the possibility of gaining the weight that you lost back.

## Thank You Page

I want to personally thank you for reading my book. I hope you found information in this book useful and I would be very grateful if you could leave your honest review about this book. I certainly want to thank you in advance for doing this.

www.ingramcontent.com/pod-product-compliance
Lightning Source LLC
LaVergne TN
LVHW021946060526
838200LV00042B/1931